10·15·81

D0732486

3 0600 00276 9132

Summer Palaces

SUMMER PALACES

Peter Scupham

Oxford   New York   Toronto   Melbourne

OXFORD UNIVERSITY PRESS

1980

Oxford University Press, Walton Street, Oxford OX2 6DP

OXFORD LONDON GLASGOW
NEW YORK TORONTO MELBOURNE WELLINGTON
KUALA LUMPUR SINGAPORE HONG KONG TOKYO
DELHI BOMBAY CALCUTTA MADRAS KARACHI
NAIROBI DAR ES SALAAM CAPE TOWN

© *Peter Scupham 1980*

British Library Cataloguing in Publication Data
Scupham, Peter
  Summer Palaces.
  I. Title
  821′.9′14   PR6069.C9   79–41263
  ISBN 0-19-211932-X

*Printed in Great Britain by
The Bowering Press Ltd, Plymouth and London*

CONTENTS

v

ACKNOWLEDGEMENTS

Some of these poems first appeared in The Mandeville Press,
Meridian, *New Poetry 4*, *Other Poetry*, *Outposts*, Peterloo Poets,
Plan, *Poetry Nation*, *The Poetry Review*, *The Starwheel Press*,
The Times Literary Supplement, *Thames Poetry*, and *Encounter*.
Megaliths and Water was first broadcast on BBC 2 'Poetry
Now', and published as a sequence by The Mandeville Press.
Natura was first published by The Gruffyground Press.

The Cart

It is, after all, only a collection of leaves.
Hours bring them together; ends are not disclosed.
There is the work of hands, felt by their absence.
        They have taught the grasses

But the lesson is lost on them. The birds, though,
Know there is something that they have to do.
It is the way heads nod; they skip the air
        Which is not warm, not cold.

Is this, then, no-place? The wind might say so
As it feels its way through trees, draws down
A gauze of dust at the turning of a path.
        The sky makes itself plain

Upon the ground, and time shapes into seasons.
Their curls are shifted over here and there.
A chrysalis is cooled to the look of life;
        Wings fix, then dry away.

Earth over earth : here is the reliquary
Closed on a wheel chipped from the children's cart.
The talismans are scattered in the courses
        By which light answered them

When secrets were kept and the maze threaded,
The garden spoke with its one feeling voice
Through flowers which denied their own corrosions
        And had no need for names.

The Chain

Above us, numbing all our dreams with tales
Of bad islands, infestations of gulls,
The metal broadsides of our great ark tower.
There hangs the chain : sealed rounds of iron
Whose chafe and rust, they say, ensure our freedom.
Paid out with its reel of swollen fathoms
Something of us gropes there, where deeper, deeper,
The hook works pain into a muddy craw.

Allow us good days, when, in certain lights,
Waves ease links to invisibility,
Gleam slips from gleam, all the lithe flexure
Polishes to a haze of blue and pearl.
So the stump dwarves, gold-beating out Sif's hair,
Worked that obdurate element to a nature
Divine and animal : this was craft-work,
A clasp tendered by their slavish hands.

Our Pilot, arms akimbo, saturnine,
Rigged out in steeple hat and greasy frock-coat,
Stares back at us from his ancestral eyes.

The Dapples

Ripples break, widen, die—the solid pool
Cradling a raft of weed whose moorings ease
To the perceptions of a glancing wind.
Algae fume greenly, coiling their suspensions
Under the tension of a cold meniscus.
The chestnut dips into the apple-tree;
Grown crisp and luminous in the sun's affection,
Fingers of leaf-work clasp and ease apart.
While water-gleams, reflected, caught and held,
Wheel free their dapples into summer air.

A dazzle-paint, confusing space and time :
Waves, rocked about their clouded chequerboard,
Slip sunlight from the backs of Seven Seas
Which blows with silver music from a bandstand,
Twirls in a reach of sunshades, loosely wavers
From the spun roundels of a playroom stove
And shakes from frocks and flowers back to sky
Whose circulations gather and deploy
These glints which still and flicker in the leaves :
Young wings of light, working to fly, fall free.

Garden Lantern

Dry garden dust, wreckage of wing and case,
    Clings to the gutter-line, the ribs and veins;
Each ancient light splits from a slate of glass
    And Moorish arches rim the cockled panes :
A dull pavilion, mossed with verdigris,
    Storing dark nonsense in its cavities.

But lanterns call the light into a round
    On rainy evenings when the clock strikes wrong;
Glossing the laurel, patching out the ground,
    They speak of clearings in a forest tongue.
A searchlight swings its throbbing disc; once more
    A cloud of wings brightens the dancing-floor.

Now all the paper lanterns float it high :
    St Elmo's fire sits roosting on the mast,
A Jovial ball of light comes hissing by,
    And kitchen-girls quake to its thunder-blast.
A Jack O'Lantern aches at your desire,
    Hovering enticements over Grimpen Mire.

The pale Victorian lovers linger on,
    Though street-lights fray and crumble at the edge;
Rough jungle tracks of tar and metal run
    Past doubtful anacondas in the hedge.
Lianas of depression and despair
    Thicken their hold by Avenue and Square.

This metal socket for the groan of wind
    Makes room for absence, draws into its space
The darkness which will never comprehend
    Whatever moved upon the water's face
Or spins the globe in stoles of smoky light
    To cold antennae homing in through night.

Lighting Rehearsal

The old Wish-house wakes into our sleep,
Creaking its giant shadows round our heads.
It is Cold Lairs, the place of dead brocade,
Illyria, lady : always some Virgin Island
Whose caverns music must enter, and define.

The four winds drowse tonight, and will not strum
Aeolian harps. Our fields, our cloths of gold,
Are tacked down gingerly. The night draws on
Into its smallest hours. We prop our eyes
Against these brittle planes of acid light.

The Doldrums, and a spread of cold canvas. Space
Chalks out its miles to Cassiopeia's Chair,
Astir with dust-motes, old theologies,
Stage armies of the good and bad whose hosts
Admit the starlight on a curving course

To wash our pitched roof in its blended silvers.
Out there, the soundless acres grow obscure;
Here, we must clarify with our rough magic
Tropics of Cancer and of Capricorn :
The Islands of the Mighty, or the Blessed.

Spirits of Place, we beat these bounds again
At intersections of mysterious shade.
The diaphragms contract, expand, and throw
Their quivering roundels to the water-floor,
Bobbles of glow which skew the shape of things

Until the darkness gathered in the wings
Lowers all colours. Omnes exeunt.
Fresnels and floods cool their bright hutches down;
Someone brings up a pre-set for the dawn.
Our country waits to find its origins.

5

Stage Wardrobe

O pearly kings and queens,
Furnish your dusty thrones
From this rag retinue.

Chasten our nostrils
With corruptions of moth,
The fumes of grave-linen.

Here we exhale the dead
Whose talk is out of season.
They cloud the rafters

Or work a slow passage
To the fluff and nothing
Of their neighbour pockets.

What poor forked animals
Will cipher out these lendings,
Supply these unfleshed creases?

Cut him down, the hanged man.
With one brief kiss of life
Send the green sap rising;

Though your pale hands, reaching,
Sharpen to bone, to zero,
And your dress, motionless,

Fixes as bright things must,
Into a charcoal shade,
A puzzle of close air.

THREE SISTERS
(For Phoebus Car)

1 The Dry Tree

Baron, as your fingers untie music,
Four seasons ebb and flow, the migrant cranes
Wind their slow skeins from climate into climate

And the dry tree shakes in its dance-measure :
Green arms, brown arms, linked in amity
Though bark strips from the cracked and polished bole.

A hover of dust : the patterned air discloses
Leaves shivered with light, gardens whose pages
Open or shut as dawn or dusk require.

But then the dissonance, the stopped movement.
The room withdraws to its four corners
And no God speaks a word of grace or power.

For now the windows thicken to a snow
Obscure and vast, with powers to impress
The old and unborn armies foundering there,

And a green Maenad dances out her frenzy
About the sapless branchwork of her fellow;
The soldiers break step on the silting road.

A dead bird, loosed from the retaining sky,
Stiffens : a twig of clouded foliage,
Eyes fathomless beneath their cooling hoods.

2 Wild Grass

In corners where a bird repeats one note
And clouds make blank faces over garden walls,
Hoisting into the blue and beyond the blue,

Time is a study in continuations.
But for you, Masha, should meaning cloud and fail,
Life, you say, becomes wild grass, wild grass.

In such corners, that is the wind's concern.
The bird repeats one note chack chack;
The wall dangles with sour and vivid cherries

Whose notes are discontinuous, abrupt.
The child at the keyboard picks, unpicks a tune,
Coding the air with lost ends and beginnings.

Here is the wild grass : a speechless city
Where threads of life are plied into a sampler.
Errands are run by the quick-dying creatures,

Each movement bright and urgent as the call-sign
Of child or bird tapping their counterpoint
Against the clock, the poppy-head's oblivion.

Listen to the soft thresh of their ground-bass,
Time and the wild grass working, this way, that way,
Their tingling feather-heads, their cutting blades.

3 *The Curving Shore*

If only we knew. The garden fills with partings,
Rustling in summer silks and coloured streamers.
The green shell brims with music, and with pain.

A dance of insects, and the sun's gold beaten
Too thin for use : from all their cooling shrines
The little gods of place absent themselves

And broken paths return upon their traces.
A hopeless fork tricks out the garden seat;
The leaves are talking in dead languages.

Cloud upon cloud, the open skies re-forming :
Their echelons move off to the horizon,
Dipping westwards over the rim of the world.

Hand falls from hand; our eyes are looking down
Long avenues of falling trees. Apart,
The maple weighs its shadow out and down

On birds caught in a cage of air and grass
At work about their chartered liberties,
On pram-tracks lining out the sullen ground,

And music silvering the middle-distance
Whose bright airs tarnish as the bandsmen play.
The soldiers pass along the curving shore.

The Tragedy Of

1

He lays a sudden anger on the table
To fester with the ink and scratchy feathers,
His treaties, proof against all our entreaties.
We dress by mirrors which contain the gardens,
But the civilities of grass and water
Are fractured by a peacock's uncouth cry,
And a slow mildew breaks the quicksilver
From that perfection which our faces claim.

The coinage rings false, the guards are doubled,
And the Fool's head sits oddly on his shoulders.
An official artist has been appointed
Who doodles wolves, devises cold insignia.

This royal daughter, unfit for the game,
Settles her face into its hurt silk look;
Gathers flowers, listens to the harsh birds.

2

Yes, things here have been tripped to motion.
The tethered trees pull the winds close about them,
And their impartial heads fly East and West
About our furious riding. Metal hulks
Groan into mud. We shall impress the scarecrows,
Leaving the seeded ground to rook and rain.
Colour drains bare, our thinning bannerets
Are rubbed sore by many fractious weathers.

Somewhere, walls are hung with noble silences,
Justice is benched beneath the apple boughs,
A green field sets clown and shepherd dancing
And herbs sleep in dreamy underworlds.

A rusty beggar sounds his call to alms
But a fresh post delays us with stale tactics.
Our lidless eyes grow bright with resolution.

3

We have scraped out support and front-line trenches
In the proud flesh; wit and wisdom thicken.
Our heads nod nothings to the duckboard floor;
The lion's teeth glaze in a last rictus.
Some mouths are swollen with a foolish gold,
Some sticky with the crumbs of creature comfort.
A Tertian Ague: we shall sweat it out—
There are no gifts which remain ungiven.

Enter the giant sloth, a shroud of fur.
Death of brain-stem, cortex. Shall we move
Beyond the play of all our swords and cancers
Into a dust, into a valiant dust?

Lie, under the graveyard's airy gabble,
Careless of new command, the wheel of men,
The nimble flags which sprig about our graves.

11

The Comedy Of

1

A fickle spring, perhaps, or when the snowflakes
Fall and fall, but cannot chill young bones:
Under Gemini, when gentry sons and daughters
Exchange their habits, and with candid eyes
Wake to the marble of an alien city.
There the piazza, and the petty hucksters
Who ply their fingers, offer varnished fruits.
A stranger takes us to a house of shadows,
But the wood beckons at the city's confines.
The lady is green-sickly; her dark velvets
Fill with stale air—better leaves new-minted
When the dull ache of love swells breast and loins.

> The song carries,
> Holds its burden lightly;
> The furred scabbards
> Close on their unstained blades.

2

Our fears compel us to this place of changes,
These rash pursuits under old stars and branches.
The Duke is arbitrary: his tongue is taut
With sentences of exile, execution.
He tugs at the false beard of his unwisdom;
The currents of our blood flow otherwise.
A cap and bells plays mockers with the birdsong
And shafts of wit fly down the woodland rides
Where every tree is blazed with verse and chapter
From Andreas Cappelanus' Rules of Love:

12

His compass needle steadying our hearts
When signposts twist like wooden weathercocks.

        The song clouds,
        Drifts into the minor;
        A quickening stream
        Breaks open our reflections.

3

The stars have set, the longest night is over.
Hound-music on the hill; in palace windows
Threads of silver primp the morning light.
Tokens are fetched, the brass-bound boxes opened;
Captains and hermits tell their tales and beads
And voices break, caught between grief and laughter.
A father weeps, dressed in his careful finery,
As we exchange contrition and forgiveness.
Wrapped in the plainest of all silks and tissues,
One broods upon the night, his lean face shifting
Between lost youth and age. Some wounds go deeper
Than our new amity can probe or cleanse.

        The song gathers.
        Dancing in linked fingers;
        For a held breath
        The shade and light are one.

Twelfth Night

Our candles, lit, re-lit, have gone down now :
There were the dry twigs tipped with buds of fire,
But red and white have twisted into air,
The little shadow stills its to and fro.

We draw familiar faces from the wall
But all is part of a dismantling dark
Which works upon the heart that must not break,
Upon the carried thing that must not fall.

Needles are shivered from the golden bough.
Our leaves and paper nothings are decayed
And all amazements of the Phoenix breed
Are cupboarded in dust, dull row on row,

While branchwork set upon a whitened ground
Climbs out into a vortex of wild flame.
The substance of this deep Midwinter dream :
A scale of ash upon a frozen wind.

Our candles, lit, re-lit, have gone down now :
Only the tears, the veils, the hanging tree
Whose burning gauze thins out across the sky,
Whose brightness dies to image. And the snow.

Drop Scene

Theatrical : burnt cork and stave,
A basket hilt, wild cave.

Along the midnight esplanade
The sea's rhodomontade

Of blam, pause, blam. Underfoot,
Concrete sings at the root.

But each enormous head of foam
Breaks in a child's dream;

Condenses to a Flying Bomb,
And still they pop and come.

That Christmas Eve, when out was blacked,
Sirens sang Heilige Nacht.

Candle in hand, I tumbled air
The full flight of the stair

My mother, in her childhood, nose-
Dived—the high-pitched fracture shows—

To frozen faces, a stunned head,
Adding my drop to the raid.

Theatre of War, signed small and clear :
EXIT (pursued by a bear).

A Warning Against Sharing the Children's Dreams

Nothing's at ease here. Great soft armchairs roll,
Tumble and toss, dancing a cosmic dance
With numbers, matchsticks, clouds : white clouds
Teased out of clouds. Lumps swell in the throat,
Tongues weigh like years and toes are as far as stars.
The road goes smooth, then jumbly : the sun is calling.
Sick and crying, a girl kneels in the hay.
The landscape smells like a pack of playing cards.

Avoid, if you can, the strangers : the one with a bag
Who slips through the night looking for specimen bones,
The gnarled and veiny plasticine man, who hops,
Then covers and clings, the three unsmiling clowns
Who drift towards you on black motorbikes.
In a cool garden, a statue turns its head,
The play of muscles creasing a marble neck;
You are drawn deep into its empty eyes.

The dark dogs snuff your trail : the heavy air
Must be pushed away with straining, helpless hands.
An eye drops out in the chase. No time to find it.
Safe, but the other one falls to the floor of a cave,
Eludes your twittering fingers. Fire from the crests
Of the beeches, driving, driving. The valley is burning;
Shops and houses yield to a torrent of cars,
Fragile buildings thrust further and further back.

Lucky to cheat the outstretched arms, arrive
With two moons, a pterodactyl, an indigo sky,
Where the blue cold water and the shallow pink
Meet in their lazy curls, and a voice reads out
From its own Bible the quiet rules of water.
Here you can walk with a kind friend, sexless, nameless,
Whom tomorrow you will remember with vague longing,
Or alone on a bare green hill feel the absence of pain.

A CAMBRIDGESHIRE CHILDHOOD

1 War Zone

The car goes wide about the bend
   Then fade, dissolve : the years rub down
The brightwork and the newest gloss
   To camouflage of green and brown.
      Under the magic apple tree
      Lie tracer and incendiary.

The tracks and half-tracks dip and sway,
   Break out their silver skirr and grind :
An endless convoy sliding past
   From fields of nowhere. Hoodman blind
      With ravishing stride moves like a ghost
      Towards an ever-burning coast.

White bulldogs cap the sentry-gate,
   And sad Italians, bound but free,
Patched out with lozenges and moons
   Dig for some pyrrhic victory.
      The camp's lines fade to a ground-plan,
      Lie Roman under shifts of rain.

The quarry lipped into the hill
   Silts up with scrub and masty beech;
Gathers on mats of dark and wet
   The spent rounds flicking from the breech.
      A pocky, tousled petrol-can
      Still justifies man's ways to man,

While osier and sallow grow
   Where diggers flay the gravel beds :
A blush of buff and emerald closed
   On belemnites with bullet-heads.
      Cold tinfoil bleaches on the hedge
      To set our pugging teeth on edge.

The windscreen vapours out with sky
   Through which, Ah God, the branches stir :
The light-washed reaches ebb away
   With Flying Fortress, Lancaster.
            A Lightning bolts the rainbow bridge,
            Sun caught on its twin fuselage—

Then the mill-stream. I overtake
   My doppelgänger cycling through
The ragged fringes of a war :
   The knowledge lost, if once we knew
            What song it was the sirens sung
            Among these cloudy trophies hung.

2 Pressed Flowers

Nothing more empty than bright space.
The wind runs down to a ploughed field,
Sings a little in cold wires.

Time enough for two boys
To pry about this chequer-board,
Hedging and ditching April into August.

First flowers work their sampler :
Pigments of sky and water
Chalked on the freshening earth.

Then sun at apogee
Glosses the full petals :
The bede-roll lengthens.

The florets picked and pressed,
Ichabod : the glory is departed.
Here are their oiled silks,

Interleaf of veils and veins,
The crinkled wafers fixed
Against our transience.

Stained to moss and ochre,
Fumitory, smoke of the earth :
Picked on my grandfather's death-day.

3 Catholic Church, Cambridge

The spire climbs out of every vertical,
Its planes of stone dizzying to an apex
Where gold might be a blush of weathercock,
A nimbus, or that stern all-seeing eye
Whose level rays pick out conspirators
In the old prayer books : a vanishing point
Where the clouds' cataract, the smarting blue
Work to one end.
                The gantry clock leans out
A giant moon-face from this Jacob's ladder,
A court of numerals, where black long-hand
Goose-steps a dead march, and the dawdling sun
Visits the houses of its zodiac.
Under the aegis of that riddling gold
The horses turn their dipping carousel;
The convicts wheel the compass of their yard.

4 Cam

And Camus, Reverend Sire, comes footing slow
And I come footing slow to Mr Finch,
His burly priest. Though innocence is proven,
The only grace to make my merit grow
Is to drown weekly, inch by turbid inch.

God has appointed him a fisher of men—
Or boys. His rod and staff, they comfort me;
He dangles a clammy harness of grey canvas
To slap a chill on my goose-pimpling skin.
The sunlight lowers, degree by dull degree.

In draughty sheds, where ancient sweat lies stale,
And towels rasp a blush on skinny backs,
We, sectaries of some depressed devotion,
Strip for the dark immersion which prevails
Against the offending Adam. Dampish tracks

Cross concrete to rough steps of slime and gloom;
Refractions break about the smoky green.
I gasp and bob like some poor hatching thing
Through turdy puff-balls and a brown-sick scum,
My mouth agape into the fly-blown skin.

Oh, Father Cam, squandering your favours on
The sparkling reaches where the long punts slide
In summery indolence from Banham's Yard,
Accept from me a larval orison,
Rolling like Phlebas on your sluggish tide.

5 *Searchlights*

Shafts of light move in the dusty woodland,
Cleaning old skulls, re-surfacing the water.
The grass responds to them; the world lays down
Bolts of shot silk beneath their feather-weight,
Cutting glass roofs against geometries
Of sunlight building between cloud and cloud.

Night turns in her bad dreams. We are alert
To hedges thickening, the trees doubtful.
Men work about the fields with quiet voices,
Forcing a ribbed eye to this polar probe.
The moths are sealed; they quicken to a tumult.
Their wing-tips bruise on walls of ice and jet.

Over these columns quarried from ghost-stone,
The temple-roof hangs weightless, packed with stars
And other wings, brightening before they die.

6 Neighbour

She stands at the fence and calls me till I come,
Mouthing a message for the wind to lip-read;
Only my name stands in the air between us.
A slattern house, reeking with dirt and music,
A compound of long grass, drawn round with wire,
A summer sky, aching with Cambridge blue—
These are the substance of her misery
Which forces through our bonded bricks and mortar.
Her son comes home on leave; the sobbing furies
Thicken at night. Our lives become a part
Of that insistent voice, those wavering grasses.
Her garden burns, the red rim eating out
A heart of black which blows to feathery ash.
Low overhead the puddering doodlebugs
Comb the cold air, each weight of random pain
Clenched tight—these trivial ganglions on the nerves
Of a slow-dying war. My mother's love
Betrays her to the ambulance, and asylum.
All the doors close, but in the silences
Her message stays. There is no way to read it.

7 Summer Palaces

How shall we build our summer palaces?
Will the girls bring us sherbet, and our gardens
Brown to the filigree of Chinese lanterns?

The Emperor speaks in a long robe of thunder,
Bruising us cloudily; his combs of rain
Dance out a dance of more than seven veils.

Islands of bird-music; storm-voices dwindle.
Across the blue, cirrus and alto-cirrus
Draw out an awning for our shade pavilion.

Swallows will sew our flying tents together.
We live as nomads, pitching idle camp
Under the white sheets blowing down the line,

Or swing on ropes to somersaults of grass.
The hasps creak upon our airy gallows,
Roofed by light, floored by a crush of earth.

The strong leaves curtain us; we know each scent,
The deep breaths taken behind swaying curtains.
We have become the citizens of green.

Our walls grow firm in fruit and knots of seed.
A dandelion clock rounds out the hour,
Blowing our time away in feathered segments.

The night lies warm upon a wall of shadows.
We lie as naked in our drifting beds
As the close moon, staining us with silver.

H.J.B.

You might have seen him turn days over,
Looking, surely, for what he was looking at
And something else that could be there besides.

Appropriately, he kept a Walker's Diary
And climbed his Indian summers out in Fahrenheit.
Winter conferred degrees on him in ermine.

Clouds of snow powder blown along the fields,
An Ecceitas of greenfly at his roses—
Shocks enough for this confessional.

In 1942 the Christmas tree
Had 20 candles. The chicken weighed 6 lbs.
The temperature rose to 38°.

The role became him : an exacting scribe
In courts where Ceres and Proserpina,
Tardy or pushful at their rituals,

Would help him pencil in another year
With a total absence of pronouns.
He balanced their accounts of fruit and flowers;

Made timely logs of each unpunctual journey.
Chalfont, Banbury and Virginia Water
Took sober burnish from his book of hours.

His family : J and C initially.
To be followed by A. There were meetings
With close colleagues such as F or D.

At the last Christmas he told us all :
'I might not be with you another year.'
Delirious, dying : 'I seem to be covered with roses.'

The Waiting Room

We lie where she lay, feel the bed conform
To a shape not ours, a flesh grown thin as air,
And open her eyes again to the ebb of day;
Hear the gulls for her, find her conversation
In the crook of a stain, the shift of an awkward board.

Here she is close to hand, the stuff of her life
Pasted into the cracks of a room where pictures
Lower their oils to the dusk, dark upon dark,
And coffins of letters crowding the wardrobe floor
Look to her coming, after this long delay.

Now, the family voices gather her in
To bear her part in all their quarrel and fabling.
Her life a diary only the dead can read,
She takes her place as a proper name among names,
And we are locked out, in this, her waiting room,

Alone with shades, and with these, her comforters :
Lotions and bibles under a mantle of dust.
Night-thoughts of bone—a polish of wavering light
Reaching to where, still at the bedside table,
Lie Wesley's Journals, The Pleasures of Old Age.

The Box

The box he held seemed lighter than itself :
A space for air, a fence of brittle slats.
Its rooms were cubicles of dusty satin
Couched on by nothings, and the painted lid
A shade for shades. Under the varnished leaves
Two lovers, poised upon an equal lawn,
Tilted absurdly one high parasol;
The crackled glaze rubbed up their house to shine
As if all summer lay about their grounds,
Shaking ephemeral birds and flowers loose
To give them close delight.

           Then, a sharp sense
Of some dead language muttered under trees
Whose veils and canopies could not set free
The halting sun : vistas of matchboard rooms
Opened, and drew him in to squares of echo.
Against their darkness wavering sheets of glass
Made gardens tremble in a slow dissolve
Or faces form and re-form in ice waters.
He turned, and felt the small thing in his hand
So much dead wood : a token of erosion,
Things falling silent, faces turned away.

South Cadbury

A kestrel backed by fitful sun
Banks down a stiffish tide of sky,
And fluent shadows drain or fill
The pleated circles of the hill,
The sapless jetsam, high and dry.

Sour brambles cling, whose nubbled reds
Light rides awash with dung and mud—
A dark look to the squandered hedge,
The daylight blunter at the edge—
October shallows into flood

And flap of air : a beer-can keens
And an inconsequential ball
Makes orange dance-about and pass
Or canters over streaming grass.
The year leans outward into fall,

And through the film a touch of chill
From harebells late and luminous :
The crackled stems are dusted down
Into that prevalence of brown
From which old news might reach to us

Of press and havoc in the wood,
Of gated contours making way
And our conjectured pain laid bare :
The talk is rustled into air
Or scrambled into stone and clay,

And indecipherable, the scrawl
Of bent or briar's epithet
For hobnails or for chivalry.
The kestrel quarries out the sky
And life contracts : its terms are met.

The Inscription

It is the absent thing; there is no key to it,
     Rather no key the day provides
When catchwords and the text make no connection,
The table lacks a leaf, and the portrait
     Ghosts out the title-page.

You could not walk to where the distance grounds it
     In gatherings of blue and grey,
Or surprise it by your subterfuge
Where planes of moisture shelve among the valleys.
     Best be the stay-at-home.

Long shadows walking in the guise of light
     Keep it a secret from the hill,
And those who may at this late hour be working
To piece the table and the cloud together
     Still find the preface missing.

It binds, bound only by its own inscription,
     Chapter and verse. On the North fells
Two soldiers of the Second Nervian
Set up their altar. Genio huius loci :
     To the Spirit of this place.

MEGALITHS AND WATER

1 Menhir

Here, in the spaces between sea and sea,
Beneath refining decibels of larksong,

Come slow abrasion, and the clout of air
Whose unfleshed energy confirms the stillness.

The spores of sage and orange lichen settle :
Will you, too, make a virtue of all weathers?

The old gardener with his apron sack
Held his tongue; the leaves conferred about him.

I, Men Scryfa, the written stone, remain.
Do you read me? Read me. Over and out.

2 Stone Row

A long alignment stumbles into cloud :
The black and bitter groyne where we too walk
And feel ourselves drawn to an element
Whose voice is siren, ineluctable.
The markers firm their roots, passing us on and by.

Our footprints lightly bruise the skin of the world,
As cold and transient as the rippled wind
Nibbling at goose-flesh. The bents, the mill of shell,
Make signs for parting. At our nostrils rises
The damp sea-smell of our mortality.

3 Circle

A constellation of rough numerals
Is grounded in the bracken's cog and mesh :
A dial face, blind to our veneration.

Time breeds its long divisions at our feet.
The stone wastes to its own self-effacement;
Night will bring her furious clouds and spirals.

Stubs of impacted fire, these terminals
Trawl their slow shadows round a demi-lune,
Responsive to the sweep of unseen hands,

And hours go shouldered on, the countless grass
Is worked through all its hidden generations,
Stitching again the questions to the answer.

4 Henge

Somewhere the flattering garden slips away,
Green filaments are dimmed, and the occluded sun
Falters and checks : the lively pith goes dry.

Then blades heel over as the wind lays down
A silver course among the winter wheat;
The tree-heads close their giant separations

And Angels, flown above a painted manger,
Dance out the roundels of their zodiac.
The air is dressed with a particular light.

Beyond the legends glowing overhead
Love speaks one spacious word from his domain
To ease an answering music out of stone.

5 Lake

The curls of leaves hold water, a mercury
Which trembles greenly and is not spilled.
The garden keeps it in forgotten jars.

Hills cradle light, lowering its multitudes
To lake and tarn. Gathered, gathering,
Held to the brim, and held beyond the brim

The miles of sun loosen their shining figures
About the shallows, come to lively rest
On shelves of darkness, and of shifting cold.

The hung cusp quivers, and a clasp of silver
Closes the fissure of twinned elements.
Our breath is taken between lung and gill.

6 River

A tress of weed is brushed along the lie
Of water following its own pursuits
Where the spring frogs clump out the flats and shallows,
Their sand-shapes mating in a drift and scrawl.

At the Mill's throat, a gravelled bull-head
Dawdles a spatulate shade. The grasses freshen.
We take presentiments of white and gold;
Life clarifies from shoals of ebony.

The river turns upon its pollard willows,
Each course cut cleanly; trickeries of light
Swing on their gimbals, these prevarications
Carried surely to the end which is no end.

7 *Estuary*

Meadows of water, where the nodding waders
Are brought to focus in a clouded glass,
And rain-shawls curtain off a dun horizon.

The casting worms tease out their tiny cairns
And voices carry over their own burdens :
Each indirection veers to indirection.

These are the silences to comb for shell :
We drag a shroud of bone from shifting sand,
A crumpled fuselage from Totes Meer,

Or find a witch staked out in her bleak pasture,
The rowers easy in their craft, the priest—
Salt words of God swell in the tilted throat.

8 *Sea*

Life, nourished from a primal green and grey,
Has logged these entries in your rolls and volumes :

Engines of plate and spar which work their passage
Over a cold brew thick with flesh and bone.

Creatures of plume and spray, their dark hulks buoyed
To those who are still busy about their dying.

One shadow mariner, who cannot anchor
Or grow to suffer the distress of landfall.

In spew and slick your ancient children gather :
Their draught of hemlock numbs you slow and through.

The Gatehouse

Late. And though the house fills out with music,
This left hand takes me down a branching line
To the slow outskirts of a market town.
We are walking to the Gatehouse. Mr Curtis
Will call me Peäter in broad Lincolnshire;
Redcurrants glow, molten about the shade,
The cows are switched along a ragged lane.
Tonight, my son tousles away at Chopin
And a grandfather whom he never knew
Plays Brahms and Schumann at the same keyboard—
Schiedmayer and Soehne, Stuttgart—
The older, stronger hands ghosting a ground-bass
Out of a life whose texture still eludes me,
Yet both hold up their candles to the night.
The Gatehouse settles back into the trees,
Rich in its faded hens, its garden privy
Sweet with excrement and early summer.
New bread and sticky cake for tea. The needle
Dances across : Line Clear to Train on Line;
The lane is music too, it has no ending
But vanishes in shifting copse and woodsmoke.
The levels cross : a light and singing wind,
Arpeggios, a pause upon the air.
The gate is white and cold. I swing it to,
Then climb between the steady bars to watch
The station blurring out at the world's end.
The wagons beat their poésie du départ;
The lamps are wiped and lit. Then we, too, go.

Signals

How could we tell the blaze, the patterans?
The chalk-marks on the self-effacing wall
Led us down Serpentine Street, and that itself
Was a true place, though less to us than some.
The barred arcades along the Brewery,
Tangy with fermentation and the dark?
A swirl of hop-scotch? But this was a thing
You could not do by numbers, so the dance
Would hurry you along some privet path,
Tying the grasses down to indirection,
Crossing your heart, laying your newest course
By pithless twigs, or when such markers failed,
Shredding a patch of paper to false snow.
It's true, return was always where it led to—
Though the trails petered out in Indian country,
And all the homing was as cats come home
Ghosting on feline automatic pilot.
As for the start of this mild wanderlust,
You could tune loosely in to that long thrill
When sound is shaken to a keen vibration
Before the engine grows along the curve,
Thrown on and caught by gantry after gantry
Down lines astounding in their verve and shine:
Empty and cold as metal in the sun.

Halt

Now, as clouds rag out over low hills,
The light sours between dead ground and water
Unfalling, about to fall. The windows work
Their shines, their dusty spaces, and we
Are gathered to this halt, where, long-uprooted,
The metal courses hold the flowers together
And a gas bauble in its Gothic cabin
Centres the sunlight. Now, that brightness moves
To open doors while shadows come to close them
Upon a sway into the tunnel's throat,
Each leather tongue tight on the stud, old smoke
Flocking its acrid wastes :
                                    a rack and slide
Where the impossible couplings work upon us.
Here, all the seats were taken long ago
And soldiers fill the night with canvas ditties,
Their pile of arms impressed upon the blind.
Somewhere, the dazing halls of terminus
Where the clock lords it with a Roman hand.
We sit it out until one point of light
Probes an untreated green into the curve.
A signal's clack stiffens to monitor—
One cellophane eye held up against a cloud
Which still has not let all its waters down.

Three Couples on the Last Train

Her drunk, petulant voice lifts the stale air,
Quivering with self-indulgence.
'All day I've tried to glow for you.'
Introspections, recriminations.
His head hangs heavy, sad.
In this intelligent, clownish face
The large eyes do not respond
To the travelling play of shades, reflections.

They look on with understanding,
Taking the ironies, in delicate amusement
Exchanging light glances
Which come to rest like birds.
These tokens show they are not threatened.
Their bodies make gentle love,
Nudging, parting,
To the carriage's uneven sway.

Head-scarved, sober,
Her worked face empty, she sleeps
A settled sleep no rhythm but her own
Can now disturb. By her side
He sits monumental, trailing a hand
Heavy with blue tattoo.
Unmoved, he looks beyond or through them
To a lit, hammering darkness.

The Site

Here stone was tackled, and the sum of labour
Handled about by long and clumsy weathers.
The mystery gathered underneath its caul,

Brimmed the dark conduits, the untiring song
Raised by processionals of blood and wine,
The unpicked rose, furled in a high window.

A life uncaught, whatever sketch-books came
To brush away dissolving rainbows, play
On figured surfaces to sound the deeps.

Enactments cloud the air. A catch of breath
And flurries of great scree bring the work down.
An absence welds its presence to the grass

As ineluctably as in Hiroshima :
Man, scored upon a retina of stone,
Struck by black radiance, light incalculable.

Horace Moule at Fordington

Distinction flowers on the darkened lawn;
    Sash windows open, the soft tassels shine
Where velvet rooms wait till the blinds are drawn
    On scents and silences. The heads incline
By their own gravitas; the tones exact
    Allegiance to a Church of England norm
Which has no need of this brief ritual act,
    This pause, outlasting all their hands perform.

Nobody smiles. They feel the sunlight there,
    Leaning across our shoulders; time unfurls
And we look back at these who look elsewhere.
    Their clericals absorb the light; two girls
Bleach out the summer from their swelling dress.
    A strength to set about the work of God,
This quiver-full of sons; quickened to bless
    Their strong maternal staff, paternal rod.

A neat, pale face, bare to the clearest bone,
    His eyes mere patches of uplifted shade,
The gifted one, the friend. And here alone
    All sight-lines meet, before the swerve and fade.
Our shadows will not press the grass apart,
    Or stir the cord on which their love is strung:
His finger still invites us to the heart,
    His throat uncut, the bastard son unhung.

Die Ahnherren

Close-lipped, severe, well-fed, Herr Doktor stares
Bleakly across a hundred or so years,
Self-centred in gilt-edged security:
A Lutheran Pastor in his gown and bands,
Partnered by mob-capped wife, pallid and angular.

The Old Ones—two awkward pieces which must fit
A complex tribal jigsaw. Some second cousin
Or genealogic frowst might, perhaps, place them.
We have no skill in family connections.
Disgraced, their custom is to face the wall.

Naming is primal. Features without vocables
Are monstrous as long men without their shadows,
And though names muster to encumber rolls,
Old churchyards, deeds, out-of-date almanacks,
No syllables we try give back identity.

Their loss is irremediable. A teasing flotsam,
Improvidently lacking who, when, where,
Riddles no serious person cares to solve,
They may, with luck, become their time's exemplars:
Minor and tongue-tied ghosts, dwellers in limbo.

To dealers, even such continuance dubious.
Gloomy, unsaleable. By this prognosis
Their stolid self-appraisal stands condemned;
Unlucky ones who chose a black profession,
A dignity which shrouds them to decay.

Moving

That is the course we shall not travel by;
The road sheers off where hedges put in doubt
A finger-post for other lights to claim.
They have moved house; we could by moving try
To work the cats' eyes home and find them out,
But all would call itself some other name

And in a slide the place goes into shade
As if a crust of nettles or old stone
Were cropping out a lost Tom Tiddler's ground;
And that sharp turn we could or should have made
Gathers a cavern look : all the unknown
And windy nothings live inside this round

Of orange lamps which underpin the cloud.
Our stake is at some crossroads far ahead,
Though clumsy tear-drops on the windscreen dim
Each destination, known or disallowed,
Each circuit flashed between the quick and dead
Or pulsing darkly like a severed limb.

NATURA

1 Water

A few glint beads, prisms of shaken life.
Against the window, fusions, intersections,
And a world whose edges have dissolved again

Under a fresh persuasion : the spring rain
Whose light cordage brings down the heavens,
Whose greys are only fitful shades of blue.

Water, whose runs are runs of broken music :
A trill played quick and far, a slow fingering
When the house lies asleep, its dream unbroken.

Or down there, on some early morning lawn,
Each web is lit and purified by dew—
No net so frail it will not gather her.

And in still flower-heads, the wax gradations,
The reach of pistil, stamen, these cool transients
Delay their globes against a film of colours.

Where cusps are strung on branch or guttering,
Distillations of thunder and of chasm,
The lineage is traced in clear succession

To those far crystals where a child, gazing,
Descried nothing but a sense of crystal
And trembled, though in the glass no shape would stir.

2 *Cottage Flowers*

Courtesies of childhood,
Their clouded whites and blues
Are restless with breath
Drawn in another country.

Light in its infancy
Knew them as visitors :
Their hold tenuous,
Their growth wayward.

Frail singletons, whose scent
Links evening, evening;
Whose names are threaded
On webs of rain and shine.

The packet breaks
Its rainbows open,
Sprinkles hard dust
On fingered ground.

And the shades follow,
Beckon from crevices :
Nodding familiars
Skilled in the one season.

Under a stone sun
They flourish, fade.
We endure the reproof
Of their knee-high conversations.

3 Sky

Seamless : a fiction of blue
Whose deception is absolute.
Only this pale inflection
Reveals the tension we are under.

Lucid as the Virgin's robe
Our garment of untextured air :
An innocence betrayed by time
Only to further innocence.

Tabula rasa. No chronicle
Of dawns or witless thunders,
Pencillings-in of larksong,
Dull scrawl of turbines.

Bombstick, meteor,
Clouds at their shape-changes—
Such clear denial
Deepens to affirmation.

Nine spheres elide :
Law consonant with justice
In the perfected stillness
Of a flying wheel.

A blue to which eyes lift
Fixed scars in constellation :
A drift of tracks, recording
Where angels fell from grace.

4 Lanes

Night, and the car poised.
Under a lunar gauze
Ash-tints, charcoal,
Cloths of scrim and velvet.

The labyrinth wakes :
A slough of dark skins,
A stretch of shadows.
She plumbs her own deeps.

Nothing, up sleeves
Cuffed by mouldering lace.
Ragged gloves haul in
A spool of light.

Brief revelations :
The air moth-flaked,
A spectral rabbit
Stuck in a white throat,

And one red planet
Steadying a compass card
Of pewter fields, deployed
In polished sequence.

The engine croons :
Rough dip and rise.
Sealed, centreless,
Time hangs by a thread.

5 *Natura*

How should her creatures best express her,
Her own brush-strokes being the more painterly?

Meads enamelled under the sun's cloisonné—
Leaf-gold laid on the still trellising—

Or sketched and frayed at every wind's decision,
Tethered grass a flail of grey and silver?

A push of wheat softens the sprawling field,
The bones' complexion, gentled into green,

Ghosting a crop whose plaits and bunches thicken
To summer, working slowly with the grain.

Savours of juice : blent acres of harvest
Come home and dry under a tawny moon.

Then the felt absence of the stubbed hedgerow :
Tans and ochres harrowed to the horizon.

Under the tides of air she breathes, exhales,
Move all nomenclatures of birth and death

Who share this ark, who ride our zodiac,
Swung on a course which seeks and makes no landfall.

Her veils disclose only what they insist on.
She works the swelling truth of these deceptions

To one great canvas, drawing our compassion :
Each atom locks upon its perfect fury.

6 Woods

Not the expanse of pine,
The Sibelius music
Whose dragging winds
Move darknesses about.

More, these stands and hangers:
Snippets of lean fur
Where the packed fields
Fall away to roads,

To be passed, repassed
In light and half-light:
The night's fullness
And the day's contraction.

Clenched on rises,
Their bent backs brushed
By feckless weathers—
Slow colours come and go.

Sun mazed in branches,
Bird-skull, beech-mast,
And the doves, who talk
A language of otherness.

Best, for the most, unvisited,
Their siren privacies
Calling to sentiments
Green, lost, deciduous.

7 Grass

Floored by tall grass,
Where greenish light
Balances about
Its fades and coruscations,

Your eyes brush
The feathered reaches:
Bodies hook and eye,
A wing-case cracks to film.

Air passes you over,
Draws to the field-edge
Slow blurs of down,
A float of sound.

Now, a long strike of heat.
The veils thicken;
Under the drowsed fringes
Earth stirs in her good dream.

And you, suspended
In that grave clasp,
Are light as the high cirrus
Yet carried further, and away.

Bound, with all travellers,
For the sack of summer palaces.
Gold thumbs to ochre.
Birds become their shadows.

8 Stubble Fires

Contours break the skin.
Acres of dust air
Drain from scraped fields :
White sheets bleaching to the hedge.

The rims harden
To bruised copper, violet,
Summer dead things,
A still shake of leaves.

East replies to West
In hems of ragged flame;
The darkening oils
Drift, merge, dissolve.

Ragnarok for the small gods.
Twilight wavers; cloaks
A shrivel of insects,
Morsels, burnt offerings.

And summer falls back, slips
Through policies of scorched earth.
Nostrils wince and prick
At charred roundels and striations.

An old ground-plan
Settles and clarifies
Land hurt and cleansed,
Picked to the black bone.

9 Frost

Arcades : a stand of silences, columnar.
Grass in her coarse furabout of silver,
Orange berries, blurred in their small shrouds—

Here are the hollows of night where the mist swarmed,
That dull annealing to a lodge of trees
Teased into shocks of wild and risen hair.

And, as we climb, pressed to a grey breast-work,
Air, poring over these chalk undulations,
Disturbing no pleat in the land's graveclothes,

Slips over lynchets cut against the light :
Rings counting out the centuries of cold.
Flesh creeps under the hoar skins of down.

Curds of ice block out each rut and furrow
The clouded rind fosters a blackened eye
Resolving nothing in its basilisk pupil,

While overhead, a scarified sun displays
A disc inscribed with no identity,
Outfacing a segment of declining moon.

Yet when the hill, tiring, inclines her head,
We find, returning, there on the scrawled hedgerow,
A few glint beads : prisms of shaken life.

The Beach

And Langland told how heaven could not keep love;
It overflowed that room, took flesh, became
Light as a linden-leaf, sharp as a needle.

Today, the stone pavilion throws a window
Into the morning, that great strength of silver
Shawled from the climbing sun, and on four children
Alive to rippled beach and rippled water
Swaying their metalled lights in amity.

Hands build an airy house of meetings, partings,
Over a confluence of the elements
Here, where there is neither sex nor name,
Only the skirmishes of dark and bright,
Clear surfaces replenished and exchanged.

Black dancing in a hall of spacious mirrors,
Far voices, and the hush of sea on sand
Light as a linden-leaf, sharp as a needle.

High Summer

High summer spills and swells.
Her airs alternately are smoothed and stirred
By collared doves and the complaints of men.
Machines prick, point and scar. Each creature's vagrant mood
Dizzies and handy-dandies. Staunching her green blood,
Self-healing, she binds up her wounds again,
Denies continuance to groan or word,
Slackens her decibels.

Perhaps our lesson is
To learn by heart her light : the dominant,
The reach on which shade flutters when hours tow
Dark over. Is the day, the night's pre-eminence
Assigned by tropical or polar temperaments ?
The chequers on the windowsill allow
An Alice eye to tease or circumvent
Their old antinomies.

About the furniture
These travelling breaths and coruscations flow
Through muted intervals of flight and rest.
Cup, wine and table's cool mosaic now invite
Us to consider well, according to our light,
Whether an action or its lack suits best
A still-life, balanced, feigning not to know
A hand, alert, unsure,

Can trick and touch this room
To a new mood; rouse pen and ink to fret,
Create a minor and a shifting scene.
What heartbeat stirs where that Corinthian Skyphos stands,
Redeemed and purposeless, stolen from votive hands,
Next to a Roman flask, whose pale sea-green,
Flaking to pearl and crusted violet,
No longer can perfume

The air? Light seeps away,
And fading colours emphasize that weight
Chafing the watcher at the barricade.
Between the first symptom and the diagnosis,
Between the faint hope and the hard heart's prognosis,
Come those considerations of the shade,
Night-thoughts which must be managed, soon or late,
With such grace as we may.

Again the shades relent:
Allow slim quarter-lights and silver gleams
Their possible, unreasonable joy.
A friend combined an iron and a river bed
And lay all summery there, his somnolent head
Tickled and cooled, the merry waters' toy,
Lapped in his rhythmic, amniotic dreams,
Mithraic and content.

Mere metaphors at play,
This shift of enmity or harmony
About the paintwork? Trees are laced with airs
Of various refinement. We are dumbly walled
By tall blue skies on which no warning signs are scrawled
Until an August cloudscape stiffly bears
Its load across; reminds us vacancy
Is execution's stay.

High summer interlude,
A calm to fear, a calm to celebrate,
When no wind stirs, nor any tongues intend
Plain questions, crooked answers. Our soliloquies
Relieve and distance all those harsh complexities
Of suffering and laughter at each end.
Now, ground is dead or holy, and we wait
Both chastened and renewed.

Song

The wind that winds the weathercock
    Pours down his golden throat;
He braves it out by shine or shock
    And plays his song by rote.
        All weathers twine away from him
        Their sweet or sour, ablaze or dim.

On parson, pedlar, man or maid
    He keeps a weather-eye,
His tail's a tumbling-bright cascade
    Where rain and rainbow fly.
        For he's the Golden Vanity
        Who spins about his thrice-times three.

The skies may beat him black and blue,
    He rides them out mast-high,
And whether weathers fly to him
    Or he makes weathers fly,
        Is held in balance by his art,
        Who knows his head-in-air by heart.

The changes ring from hour to hour,
    The bell-notes ply, reply;
Planted upon a shifting tower
    And in a shifting sky
        His weathers, too, will serve our turn,
        His sunlight cool, his showers burn.